Usborne
First Sticker Book
Pets

Illustrated by Manuela Berti

You'll find all the stickers at the back of the book.

Words by Kristie Pickersgill
Designed by Kirsty Tizzard

At the pet shop

It's a busy day at the pet shop, with lots of people buying things for their furry friends. Fill the shelves with tasty food, squeaky toys, comfy beds, and more.

Find an amazing hamster house to stick here.

Playtime

From a tiny Chihuahua to a giant Saint Bernard, all kinds of dogs are having fun at the play park. Fill the picture with playful pups.

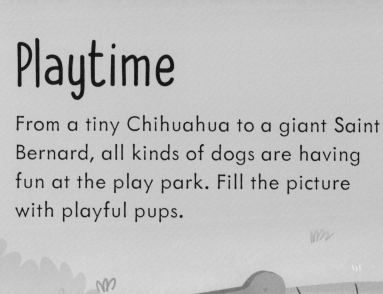

Add two more soggy dogs splashing in the pool.

When dogs bow to each other, it means they want to play. Find a pair of bowing dogs to go here.

Hamsters

This hamster mamma has babies to look after. Find six little hamsters to add to the picture. Soon they'll be ready to go to new homes.

Can you find a hamster in a wheel?

Add a hamster peeping out of the tube.

6

Guinea pigs

When the weather is nice, guinea pigs love to play and explore outside. Add more fluffy guinea pigs to the pen.

Guinea pigs like to eat dandelion leaves and flowers. Stick some nibbling guinea pigs here.

Cool cats

Some pets live in an animal shelter until a family adopts them. Today, the cats at the shelter are having fun in the playroom. Stick on some cats jumping, stretching, and snoozing.

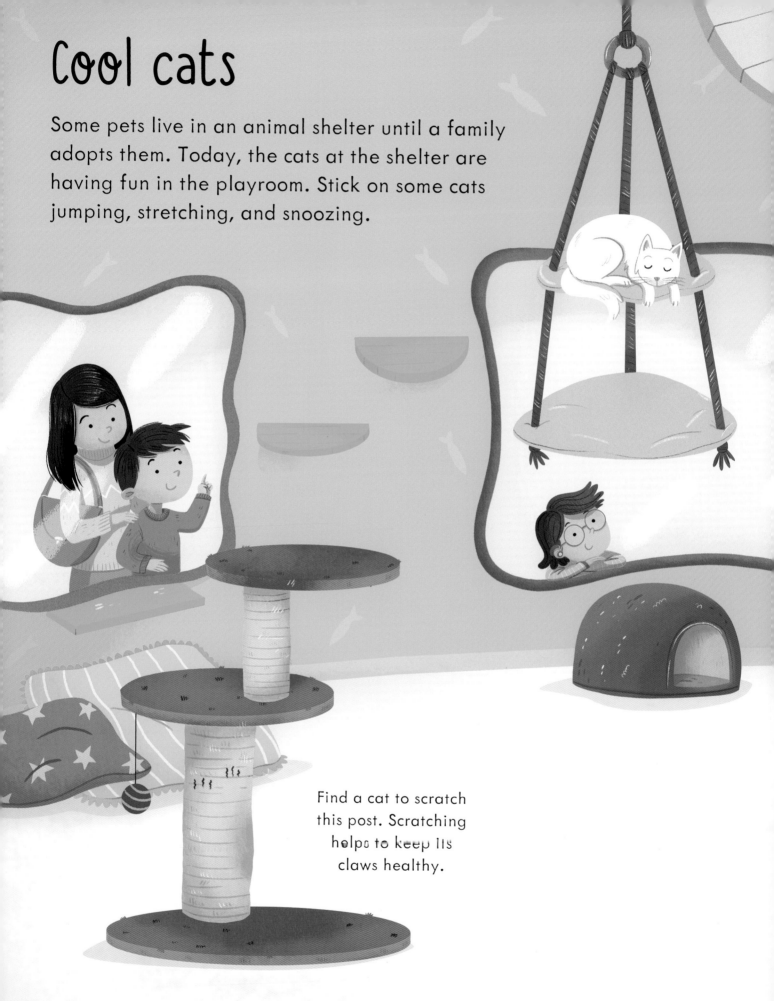

Find a cat to scratch this post. Scratching helps to keep its claws healthy.

Stick a cat with
a fluffy tail on
the walkway.

Reptile house

Not all pets are furry or fluffy, some have scales instead. Find four reptiles to stick on this page.

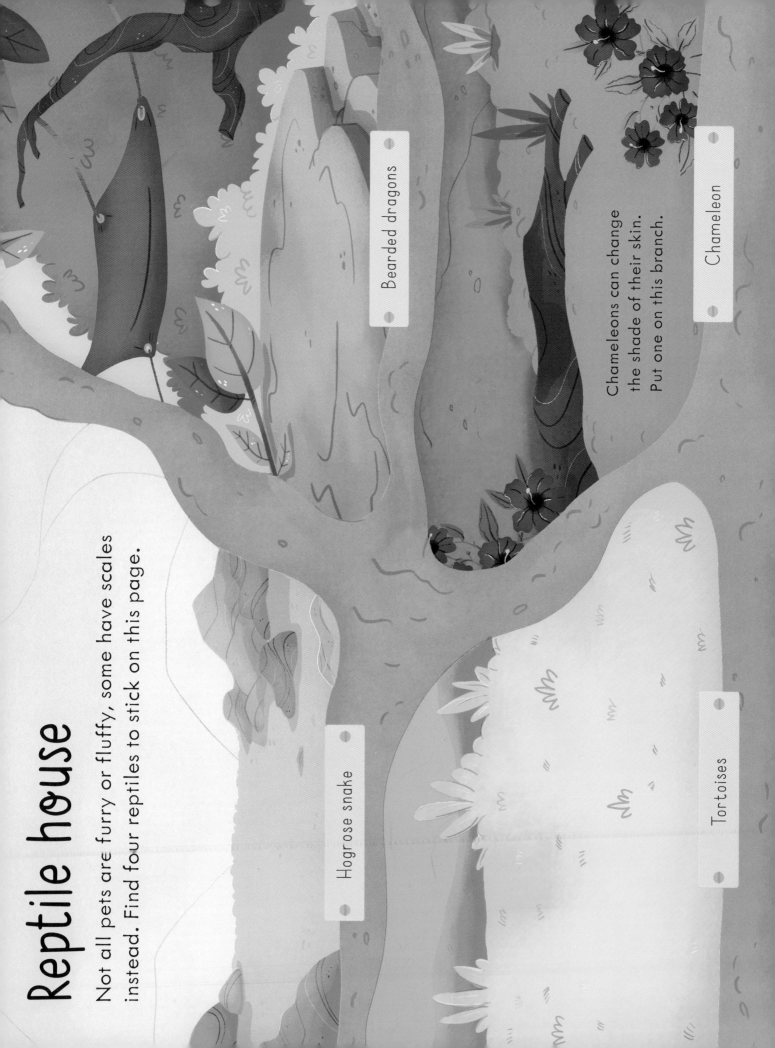

Bearded dragons

Chameleons can change the shade of their skin. Put one on this branch.

Chameleon

Hogrose snake

Tortoises

Aquarium

Add lots more bright fish to the tank.
Some are bold and brave, while others
hide between the plants and rocks.

Stick on a
goldfish peering
out of the
shipwreck.

Pets on the farm

There are so many animals to visit at the farm, from hopping bunnies to friendly goats. Stick on lots of different animals and people.

A baby goat
is called a kid.
Stick one here.

13

Visiting the vet

When pets are unwell they need to see the vet, who will help them get better. Fill the waiting room with all kinds of pets and their families.

Find a dog and cat being helped by the vets
and stick them in these rooms.

All kinds of pets

Match each sticker to the shapes on this page to discover even more pets. Which would you choose?

Mouse

Stick insect

Budgie

Tarantula

Gerbil

Corn snake

Giant snail

Stick a red-eyed frog on this rock.

Chinchilla

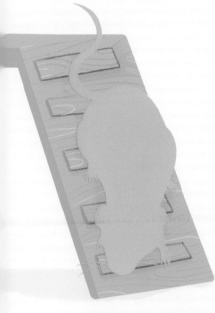

Rats are very agile. Add one to this ladder.

Gecko

16

At the pet shop pages 2–3

Grooming room

Squeaky toys

Bouncy balls

Ruff ruff

Meow

Scratching posts

Cat bed

Hamster house

Pet food

Food bowls

Playtime pages 4–5

Dachshund

Chihuahua

Saint Bernard

Greyhound

Dalmatian

Hamsters page 6

Swing

Wheel

Water

Food

Guinea pigs page 7

Water

Dandelion

Cool cats pages 8-9

Food

Toys

Reptile house page 10

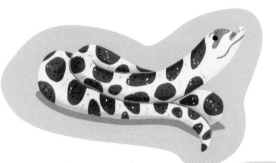

Hognose snake

Bearded dragons

Chameleon

Tortoises

Aquarium page 11

Goldfish

Guppies

Zebrafish

Pets on the farm pages 12–13

Ponies in the stable

Geese

Pony

Ducks

Hay

Chickens

Don't forget...
WASH HANDS!

Rabbits

Goats and kids

Visiting the vet pages 14–15

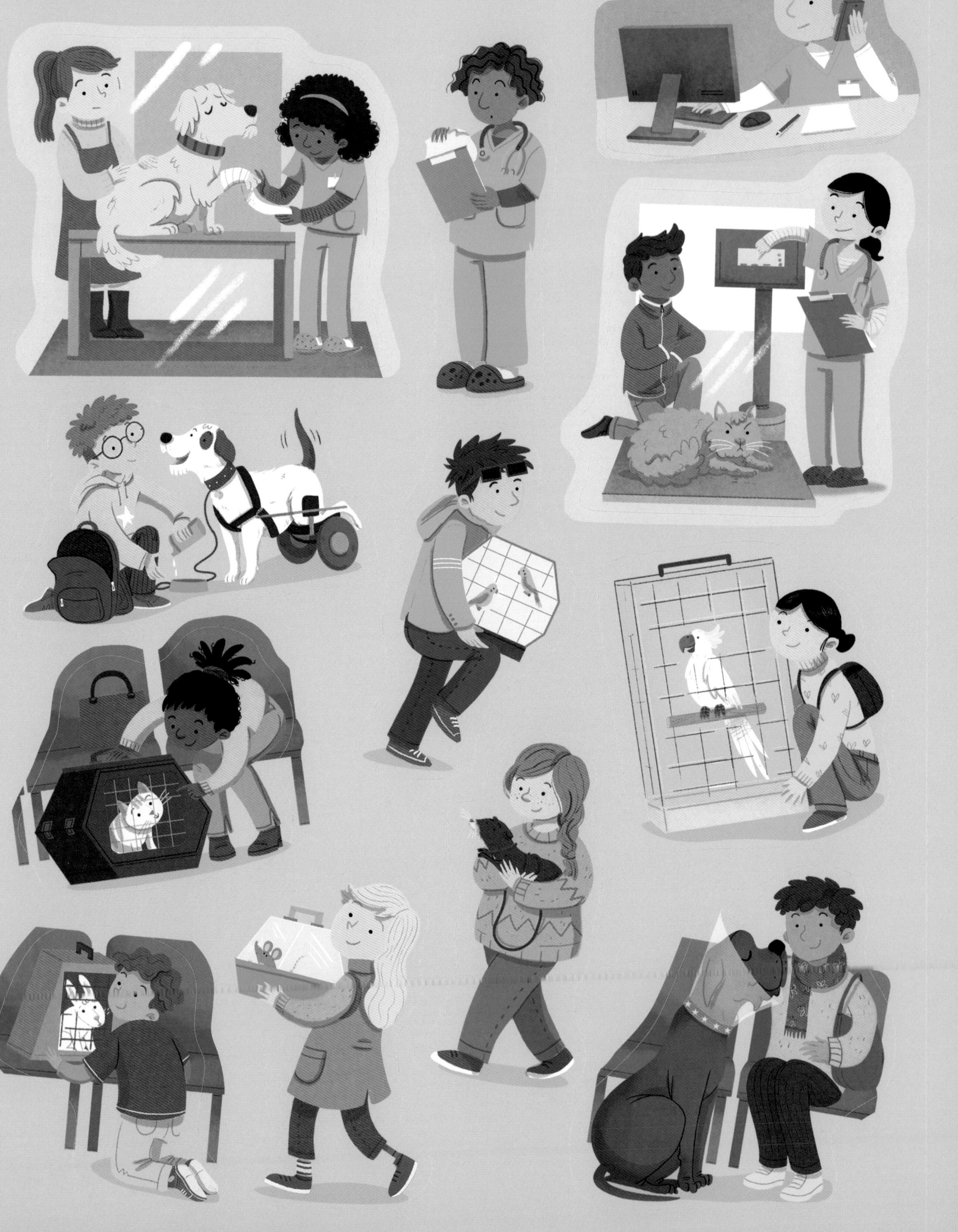

Stick insect

Budgie

Mouse

Tarantula

Gerbil

Corn snake

Giant snail

Chinchilla

Gecko